The Natural World
SOUTH AMERICA

Lyn Sirota

MEDIA ENHANCED BOOKS

AV²
BY WEIGL™

ADDED VALUE • AUDIO VISUAL

www.av2books.com

AV² provides enriched content that supplements and complements this book. Weigl's AV² books strive to create inspired learning and engage young minds in a total learning experience.

Your AV² Media Enhanced books come alive with...

Audio
Listen to sections of the book read aloud.

Key Words
Study vocabulary, and complete a matching word activity.

Go to **www.av2books.com**, and enter this book's unique code.

Video
Watch informative video clips.

Quizzes
Test your knowledge.

BOOK CODE

K 2 0 8 1 9 7

Embedded Weblinks
Gain additional information for research.

Slide Show
View images and captions, and prepare a presentation.

AV² by Weigl brings you media enhanced books that support active learning.

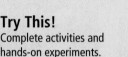

Try This!
Complete activities and hands-on experiments.

... and much, much more!

Published by AV² by Weigl
350 5th Avenue, 59th Floor
New York, NY 10118
Websites: www.av2books.com   www.weigl.com

Library of Congress Cataloging-in-Publication Data
Sirota, Lyn A., 1963- author.
 South America / Lyn Sirota.
   pages cm. -- (The natural world)
 Summary: "South America is located southeast of North America. The landscapes of South America range from mountains to rivers and deserts. Learn more about this exciting environment in South America. This is an AV2 media enhanced book. A unique book code printed on page 2 unlocks multimedia content. This book comes alive with video, audio, weblinks, slide shows, activities, hands-on experiments, and much more."-- Provided by publisher.
 Includes index.
 ISBN 978-1-4896-0958-8 (hardcover : alk. paper) -- ISBN 978-1-4896-0959-5 (softcover : alk. paper) -- ISBN 978-1-4896-0960-1 (single user ebk.) -- ISBN 978-1-4896-0961-8 (multi user ebk.)
1. Natural history--South America--Juvenile literature. 2. Ecology--South America--Juvenile literature. 3. South America--Environmental conditions--Juvenile literature. I. Title.
 QH111.S57 2014
 578.098--dc23
                         2014004675

Printed in the United States of America in North Mankato, Minnesota
1 2 3 4 5 6 7 8 9 0 18 17 16 15 14

042014
WEP150314

Editor: Heather Kissock
Design: Mandy Christiansen

Every reasonable effort has been made to trace ownership and to obtain permission to reprint copyright material. The publishers would be pleased to have any errors or omissions brought to their attention so that they may be corrected in subsequent printings.

Weigl acknowledges Getty Images as its primary image supplier for this title.

Contents

Welcome to South America!

South America is the fourth largest continent in the world. It is often referred to as a place of extremes. It has the Amazon, the world's largest river, as well as the Atacama Desert, the world's driest region. Its Andes Mountains are the longest mountain range in the world. Mainly located in the Southern Hemisphere, South America lies between the Atlantic and Pacific Oceans. It has an area of 6,880,706 square miles (17,820,947 square kilometers) and a population of 386,000,000 people.

South America has many different environments and a rich diversity of plant and animal life. Its **rainforests** have more kinds of plants than any other place in the world. Several varieties of rainforest plants are used in medicines to fight malaria, a disease spread through the bite of an infected mosquito. The Amazon rainforest alone is estimated to have more than two million **species** of insects and spiders. Animals that originated in South America include sloths, anteaters, and armadillos.

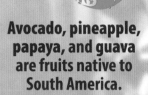

Avocado, pineapple, papaya, and guava are fruits native to South America.

One tree in the Amazon rainforest has more ant species than all of Great Britain.

Only female mosquitoes bite humans. They need human blood to develop fertile eggs.

Jaguars can be found in the dense foliage of the South American rainforests. The forests provide the cover the jaguars need to stalk prey animals.

Unique South American Life

South America has an impressive collection of animals, plants, birds, and insects. Many of these plants and animals are **endemic**. The Galapagos Islands and the Amazon rainforest are just two areas where endemic species can be found.

The Amazon rainforest contains at least 10 percent of the world's **biodiversity**. This area is home to almost 14,000 species of endemic plants, 138 endemic mammal species, 204 endemic amphibian species, and 59 species of endemic reptiles. In addition, the Amazon River contains the largest number of freshwater fish species in the world.

The Galapagos make up an **archipelago** off the northwest coast of South America. They are part of Ecuador. The environment in the Galapagos is different from other islands due to their nearness to the equator.

In the Galapagos, nearly 80 percent of birds living on land, 97 percent of reptiles and land mammals, and more than 30 percent of the plants are endemic. Some examples of endemic animals include giant Galapagos tortoises, marine iguanas, flightless cormorants, and Galapagos penguins.

Galapagos tortoises can weigh up to 500 pounds (227 kg) and live for more than 100 years.

The Galapagos

Galapagos   South America

This archipelago is made up of 13 large islands and 7 smaller ones.

Booby birds are clumsy and get their name from the Spanish word *bobo*, which means *"clown."*

With only 350 birds, the Galapagos flamingo population is the world's smallest.

The Galapagos are home to more than 50,000 Galapagos sea lions.

50 Land iguanas can live for more than years.

Galapagos penguins are the only penguins that live at or just above the equator.

Where in the World?

South America is located southeast of North America. It is connected to North America by the Isthmus of Panama. The bodies of water surrounding South America are the Caribbean Sea to the north, the Atlantic Ocean to the east and the Pacific Ocean to the west. The Drake Passage is a waterway that lies between South America and Antarctica. The equator crosses the countries of Brazil, Colombia, and Ecuador.

The climate near the equator is warm and humid, with mild winters. Rain can be heavy in the low-lying jungle areas. In the winter, the temperature drops only a few degrees, but farther south, there is more of a difference. Winters are cooler in the southern plains, valleys, and coasts. Cold winds from Antarctica bring snow and colder weather in this area.

South American Biomes

Biomes are regions of the world with similar climates, animals, and plant groups. The geography and weather determine the kinds of life that can survive in a region. The living things have similar characteristics that enable them to **adapt** and thrive in each biome's environment.

There are two classes of biomes—land and aquatic. Aquatic biomes can be freshwater or marine. South America has several land biomes. These include rainforest, deciduous forest, desert, grassland, tundra, and chaparral. The variety of biomes on the continent accounts for the diversity of its plant and animal life.

The Pampas grasslands stretch from the Atlantic coast to the foothills of the Andes Mountains.

Map of South American Biomes

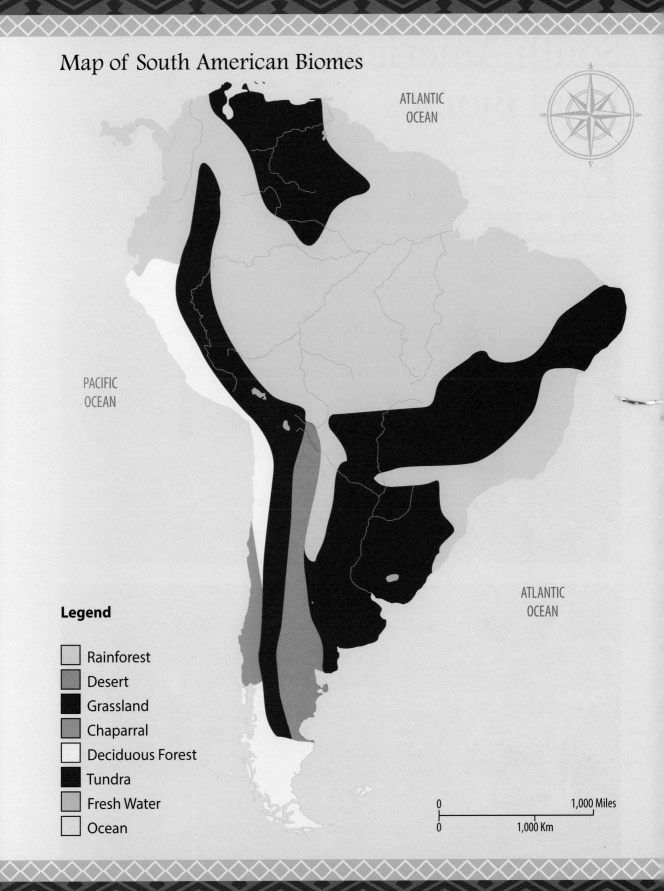

ATLANTIC
OCEAN

PACIFIC
OCEAN

ATLANTIC
OCEAN

Legend

- Rainforest
- Desert
- Grassland
- Chaparral
- Deciduous Forest
- Tundra
- Fresh Water
- Ocean

0   1,000 Miles

0   1,000 Km

South American Land Biomes

Each type of biome has a different set of characteristics. The biomes in South America all have similar characteristics to the same biomes on other continents. The types of animals and plants that live in these biomes also share similar traits.

Rainforest

Rainforest biomes are known for their tropical climate and plentiful rainfall.

Plants: The rainforest is a fertile environment, where high treetops close off the sunlight. More than 2,500 kinds of trees can be found in the Amazon rainforest.

Animals: Birds, mammals, reptiles, and insects can be found at various levels of the rainforest, from the forest floor to the **canopy**.

Average Temperature 75°F (23.8°C)

Rainfall 80 to 300" (203 to 762 cm)

Desert

The desert biome is dry. Days are hot and sunny, while the nights are cool.

Plants: Desert biomes have few plants due to the lack of rain. Grasses, ferns, and cacti grow on sandy hills. Some plants grow on bare soil but are not rooted to the ground. They tumble across the desert.

Animals: The animals that inhabit this biome have adapted to extreme temperatures and the lack of water. Scorpions, insects, lizards, and some rodents can survive in the desert. Armadillos, llamas, foxes, and eagles can also be found here.

Day 32 to 77°F (0 to 25°C)
Night 10 to 15°F (−12.2 to −9.4°C)

Rainfall Less than **24"** (61 cm)

Every biome is different in its own way. Species that are common to a biome in one area may be different from the same biome in another. For example, there are specific plants that live in the Amazon rainforest that cannot survive in the Indo-Malaysian rainforest.

Grassland

Grasslands are large, wide areas of grass and plants. They are transition zones between deserts and forests. In South America, they are also referred to as savannas.

Plants: Sprawling grasslands are filled with trees, shrubs, and grasses. In the tropical savanna called the Llanos, swamp grass, sedges, and carpet grass grow along with the Llanos palm tree and scrub oak.
Animals: The largest snake in the Americas, the anaconda, lives in this biome, along with birds such as storks, ibises, and herons. The capybara, known as the world's largest rodent, also resides here.

Winter
Average **65°F**
(18°C)
Summer
above **80°F**
(26.6°C)

Rainfall
55"
(140 cm)

Chaparral

South America's chaparral biome is found on the continent's southwest coast. Chaparral biomes are known for their hot, dry summers and cool, wet winters.

Plants: The plant life in this biome is diverse. Orchids grow in this area along with rock roses, strawberry tree shrubs, and carob trees.
Animals: Rodents are plentiful in this biome, as well as the raptors that hunt them. These raptors include eagles and kestrels. Many kinds of reptiles can also live in this biome.

Winter
35 to 60°F
(1.6 to 16°C)
Summer
Average **72°F**
(22.2°C)

Rainfall
11 to 35"
(28 to 90 cm)

South American Ecosystems and Habitats

Every biome is made up of many different ecosystems. Ecosystems are the communities of plants, animals, and other living things that populate an area. These populations feed, reproduce, and interact with each other in the same environment. Ecosystems can vary in size. They can be as small as a single tree or as large as a forest. The living things in an ecosystem are dependent on each other and their environment for food and shelter.

An ecosystem is made up of **habitats**. A habitat is where a specific species of plant or animal lives. The main elements of a habitat are food, water, shelter, and space. Similar to ecosystems, habitats can range in size. South America is known for its unique ecosystems and habitats.

The Amazon region has the largest rainforest in the world. The rainforest has trees almost 100 feet (30.5 m) high. Birds of prey such as the harpy eagle build their nests in the canopy. These **predators** hunt animals such as parrots, monkeys, and sloths.

The Atacama Desert extends for 600 miles (966 km) along the west coast from Peru to northern Chile.

The Atacama Desert is found along the coast of Chile. Parts of the desert get almost no rain at all. **Lomas** grow on bare soil but do not root. Vampire bats and two species of foxes live among the lomas.

The Llanos is a tropical grassland bordered by the Andes Mountains. During the rainy season, the capybara dines on the plentiful grasses and aquatic herbs that are part of this biome.

The Pantanal is the world's largest freshwater wetland ecosystem. It is located in the floodplain of the Paraguay River. During the dry season, the Pantanal is home to 656 bird species and more than 100 mammal and reptile species.

The rhea, a flightless bird, lives in the South American grasslands. With its long and powerful legs, it can run quickly and see over tall grasses.

Plant Life in South America

The plants of South America are as different as the biomes. The plant life of the grasslands is a mix of herbs, grasses, bamboo, and deep-rooted trees. Cacti are common in the desert because they can store water. The rainforest biome is known for its numerous and varied plant species. Two and one half acres (1 hectare) of rainforest can contain as many as 750 species of trees and 1,500 species of **vascular** plants. In the chaparral biome, there are approximately 25,000 species of plants. They are well adapted to extreme heat, cold, and drought.

Bamboos are evergreens. This means they keep their green leaves all year.

Bamboo

Bamboo is a tree-like member of the grass family. It grows quickly, branching from thick underground stems. A few species have been known to grow as much as 39 inches (99 cm) in one day. Most bamboo species take 12 to 120 years to flower.

Copiapoa Cactus

The Copiapoa cactus is adapted to the harsh environment of the Atacama Desert. This desert is close to the ocean, and fog forms where cold ocean water meets the warm wind of the desert. Copiapoa cacti can absorb water vapor through their leaves. The cacti also form "rain roots" that grow within hours of rainfall These roots absorb the water. They then die when the soil dries.

The Copiapoa is named after the town of Copiapo in Chile. These cacti vary in size from single spherical plants to massive clumps.

Liana

Lianas are long, woody vines that some animals use to swing through the rainforest. Lianas root in the forest soil and wind around other plants as they grow skyward. They can grow up to 330 feet (101 m) high around trees that support them. They produce flowers at different time periods and provide a food source for animals.

Lianas will sometimes wind around themselves to grow toward the light.

Orchid

More than 100 species of orchids grow in South America's chaparral biome. Orchids grow well in warm, open spaces. This enables them to attract insects and birds, which are critical to the **pollination** process. Some orchid flowers mimic female insects in color, scent, and shape. This prompts male insects to transfer pollen between orchid plants.

Orchids have bilateral symmetry. If a line were to be drawn down the middle of the flower, the two sides would be mirror images of each other.

Just the Facts

The Puya raimondii is a rare plant from the Andes that only flowers on its 100th birthday.

The Chilean palm, harvested for its syrup and nuts, is only found in national parks.

2 out of 3 plant-based pharmaceutical drugs come from plants in the Amazon.

The Cerrado, part of the Brazilian highlands, has more than **10,000** *species of herbs and grasses.*

Insects, Reptiles, and Amphibians

South America has a plentiful collection of insects, from leaf-cutter ants, stag beetles, and termites to butterflies, dragonflies, and mosquitoes. They are an important food source for the many reptiles and amphibians that inhabit the continent. Turtles, lizards, crocodiles, and snakes crawl, skitter, and slither through their habitats. Amphibians, such as frogs, toads, and salamanders, live on land and in water.

When the morpho flies, its coloration makes it look as if it is appearing and disappearing. This allows it to hide from predator birds, such as the jacamar and flycatcher.

Blue Morpho

The blue morpho butterfly is known for its size and iridescent blue color. Morphos range from 5 to 8 inches (13 to 20.3 cm) in length and spend most of their time on the rainforest floor. When looking for mates, they will search all parts of the forest. Adult morphos drink juice from rotting fruit, tree sap, fungi, and wet mud.

Green Anaconda

The green anaconda lives in and around rivers in South America. An anaconda can be more than 30 feet (9.1 m) long, 12 inches (30.5 cm) in diameter, and weigh more than 550 pounds (250 kg). It often grabs its prey when the animals come to the river to drink. This snake wraps itself around its prey to suffocate it. It then swallows the animal whole. Green anacondas can eat large animals such as deer, sheep, and caiman.

Adult green anacondas have no natural predators, but young snakes are easy prey for other reptiles, birds, and mammals.

Poison Dart Frog

Poison dart frogs are known for their bright colors. These frogs can be red, blue, green, black, copper, yellow, or a mix of these colors. Though beautiful, the colors signal danger to predators. The poison dart frog stores venom in its skin that can paralyze or kill a predator. This reptile eats ants and small insects.

Poison dart frogs are quite small, growing only 1 to 2 inches (2.5 to 5 cm) long.

Marine Iguana

One of the many unique animals of the Galapagos Islands, the marine iguana sneezes frequently to expel salt from the glands near its nose. It uses its sharp teeth to eat algae and seaweed off rocks. On average, the iguana lives 5 to 12 years and does not have many natural predators. Young iguanas are prey for hawks and other seabirds.

The marine iguana can remain underwater for up to 45 minutes or until it can no longer handle the cold temperature.

Just the Facts

The goliath bird eater, the largest spider in the world, measures up to 12 inches (31 cm) long and bites prey with its large fangs.

The life span of a blue morpho is only about 115 days.

Scientists believe the first tortoises came to the Galapagos 2 to 3 million years ago.

A green anaconda can lunge toward its prey at a speed of 20 feet (6.1 m) per second.

The venom of the golden poison dart frog is strong enough to kill 10 humans.

Birds and Mammals

South America is sometimes referred to as the "bird continent." Nearly 3,000 species of birds can be found there. Many native birds from the rainforest regions are brightly colored, such as the macaws, parrots, toucans, and parakeets. Mammals are another diverse part of the animal population. Large mammals, such as jaguars, llamas, bears, tapirs, and wolves, roam different habitats. Smaller mammals, such as monkeys, sloths, otters, ocelots, and armadillos, are also found on the continent. Jaguars prey on both small and large mammals, while smaller mammals may prey on insects or just forage plants. Each animal, no matter how large or small, plays an important role in its environment.

With a wingspan of about 10 feet (3 m), the Andean condor is one of the world's largest birds of prey.

The Andean Condor

The Andean condor lives in the Andes Mountains. It feeds on the remains of dead animals, using its curved, sharp beak and claws to remove the flesh. Unlike other birds, the Andean condor does not build nests. The female condor lays eggs in caves or holes. These hiding places keep predators away so the chicks are protected.

Vampire Bat

Vampire bats are the only mammals that feed entirely on blood. The bats have heat sensors on their noses that enable them to locate resting animals while flying at night. The vampire bat often feeds off the blood of livestock. When the vampire bat bites its prey, the bat's saliva prevents the blood in the wound from clotting. The bat drinks the blood as it flows from the wound.

Like other bat species, vampire bats live in colonies.

Jaguar

The jaguar is the largest cat in South America. It is an impressive hunter and will climb trees and jump rivers to find its prey. Most jaguars are found in the Amazon region. They live an average of 12 to 15 years.

Jaguars can weigh from 100 to 250 pounds (45 to 113 kilograms).

Marmoset

Marmosets are some of the world's smallest monkeys. One variety, called the pygmy marmoset, is only 6 inches (15 cm) long and weighs only about 3 ounces (85 g). The marmoset lives along rivers and in tropical forests. It uses its long tail for balance when moving through the trees.

The marmoset chews holes into tree bark to lick the sap that flows from the wound.

Just the Facts

The giant hummingbird of Chile is 8.5 inches (21.7 cm) long and is the largest hummingbird in the world.

South America is home to about 7 million llamas and alpacas.

The tapir, the Amazon rainforest's largest mammal, has a trunk like an elephant, only shorter.

Three-toed sloths spend 80% of their time napping in the trees of the rainforest.

A jaguar has the strongest bite force of all cats.

South American Aquatic Biomes

In addition to the land biomes, South America has two aquatic biomes, freshwater and marine. The main difference between the two is the level of salt in the water. Marine biomes have about one cup of salt for every gallon (4 liters) of water.

Aquatic Ecosystems and Habitats

Aquatic ecosystems and habitats are rich in plant and animal life. Freshwater ecosystems exist in rivers, streams, lakes, and ponds. The mighty Amazon River has 1,000 tributaries, or feeder streams, that drain into its 3,900-mile (6,276-km) stretch of waterway. This river accounts for one-fifth of all the river water on Earth. The flow rate of the river varies, which creates different environments. For example, fast-moving water picks up more nutrients, oxygen, and carbon dioxide, making it a thriving ecosystem.

Freshwater Biome

Rivers, lakes, streams, ponds, and wetlands are all part of South America's freshwater biome. The amount of water in these inland water sources depends on rainfall and the climate of the regions where they are located. The levels of the Amazon River change depending on the season. The plants and animals in this ecosystem depend on the water to survive.

Plants: Water lilies, grasses, ferns, and lotuses grow in South America's freshwater biome.

Less than 1% salt content

Animals: Plankton, fish, frogs, mayflies, black flies, and salamanders are found in and around the waters of the freshwater biome.

The oceans around South America also contain many ecosystems. Each ecosystem is defined by factors such as the weather, tides, wind, sunlight, and circulation. **Coral reefs** are popular habitats in the tropical regions. They provide shelter and food for many varieties of fish, sponges, anemones, and algae. **Mangrove** forests and sea grass beds are also popular environments for sea life such as oysters, mussels, barnacles, seahorses, shrimp, and lobsters. Most living things eat well in this nutrient-rich environment.

The root system of the mangrove tree helps prevent coastal erosion during storms.

Marine Biome

With oceans on either side of South America, the marine biome is a vast one. Underwater reefs, forests, and grass beds provide many areas for animals to eat, hunt, reproduce, and hide from predators. Mangrove forests along coastal areas are habitats for insects, spiders, and crustaceans. Even larger grazing animals such as pigs and antelope roam mangroves forests looking for food.

Plants: Seaweed, algae, and sea grass are some of the vegetation found in South America's marine biome.

Animals: Fish, dolphins, manatees, whales, sharks, sea cucumbers and sea urchins make their home in this aquatic biome.

About 3% salt content

South American Aquatic Life

Both marine and freshwater plants and animals must have their basic needs met in an environment in order to survive. Through **photosynthesis**, marine plants and algae provide oxygen and take in large amounts of carbon dioxide. Most organisms need oxygen to live. Although algae is found in both freshwater and marine biomes, most plants are specific to one biome. Marine birds, such as gulls and pelicans, spend their lives in saltwater habitats. Many mammals, including pacas and capybaras, spend their time in and around fresh water.

A piranha has a long, thin body that may be green, brown, black, or silvery blue.

Piranha

The piranha is about 8 to 18 inches long (20 to 46 cm), with triangular, razor-sharp teeth. A piranha will attack and chew any living animal, including other piranhas, small fish, and humans. It also eats seeds and fruit, as well as anything else that falls into the water.

Amazon River Dolphin

The Amazon River dolphin lives in both the Amazon and Orinoco Rivers. It has light skin that appears as different shades of pink. This type of dolphin is approximately 6.5 feet (1.98 m) in length and is known to turn bright pink when it is excited. It has bristly hairs at the end of its snout to help it search muddy river bottoms for food.

Unlike most dolphin species, the Amazon River dolphin can turn its neck from one side to the other.

Sea Cucumber

Common to the marine biome, the sea cucumber is a soft-bodied **echinoderm** that lives near the ocean floor. It ranges in size from 0.75 inches to 6.5 feet (2 to 198 cm). The sea cucumber eats aquatic animals and tiny particles of algae. There are approximately 1,250 known species of sea cucumbers in the world.

When threatened, some sea cucumbers shoot out sticky threads to distract the enemy. Others release their internal organs, which are later regenerated.

Flightless Cormorant

The flightless cormorant is an endemic species of bird that lives only in the Galapagos on Fernandina and Isabela Islands. With a population of only about 1,600, it is considered one of the world's rarest birds. The flightless cormorant lives in colonies, or groups. It depends on eels, octopuses, and fish from the ocean for food. While searching for food, it does not venture very far from the colony.

The flightless cormorant weighs between 5.5 and 11 pounds (2.5 and 5 kg). It is the heaviest of all cormorant species.

Just the Facts

*The Amazon River dolphin has a **brain capacity 40% larger** than that of humans.*

The Amazon rainforest includes more than 1,000 rivers.

There are more than 10,000 different species of seaweed in South America.

A piranha's jaw is so strong that it can crush a human hand within 10 seconds.

Maintaining Balance

Ecosystems consist of both living and non-living things. Every part of an ecosystem is interdependent, so even small changes can affect the populations that live there. For example, if the water levels in an aquatic environment change, algae growth can be affected. This, in turn, affects the available food supply for some animals. Smaller algae populations can reduce the oxygen level of the water. The plant and animal life that live in that water may not have sufficient oxygen to breathe. Balance is critical for the care and maintenance of a thriving ecosystem.

Introducing New Species

There are times when a new or non-native species is introduced to an ecosystem. The result can be dramatic. Often, the new species will have no natural predators. The population of the new species will continue to grow and compete for resources, which alters the natural balance of the ecosystem. In the 1930s, red fire ants found their way onto a U.S. ship leaving Brazil. When the ship docked in Alabama, the fire ants made their way to land. These ants were highly destructive and hard to control. This species is aggressive to humans, livestock, pets, and wildlife, causing painful bites.

Red fire ants pose a health issue. They swarm and relentlessly sting anything that disturbs them.

Ecosystem Interactions

All organisms in an ecosystem interact with each other. They are each part of a food chain. Every food chain contains producers, primary and secondary consumers, and decomposers. Producers are plants that use the Sun's energy to make food. Primary consumers are herbivores that eat plants. Secondary consumers feed on herbivores. Decomposers break down dead organisms and return nutrients to the soil.

Ants & Termites
Ants and termites are decomposers. They eat dead plants and trees, including the Brazilian nut tree. These insects provide food for anteaters.

Anteaters
The anteater sticks its long snout and tongue into anthills and mounds to eat ants and termites. Agoutis bury food in the holes made by anteaters.

Brazilian Nut trees
Brazilian nut trees are producers. They depend on agoutis to spread their seeds. Without agoutis, new Brazilian nut trees would not sprout.

Agoutis
Agoutis are rainforest rodents that use their sharp teeth to eat Brazilian nuts. They are primary consumers. Carnivores such as jaguars and pumas eat agoutis.

Jaguars
Jaguars are secondary consumers. They eat the agouti, capybara, tapir, and fish. Jaguars hunt and rest under the shade of Brazilian nut trees.

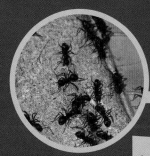

Diversity and Humans

The diversity of South American ecosystems is important for everyone. As the home of the world's largest tropical rainforest, this region provides oxygen, clean water, shelter, and food. The plants of the rainforest also supply important treatments in medicine. Scientists are still discovering species in the rainforest that may hold the key to curing diseases. Pharmaceutical companies use many plants, native to this region, in creating products that help people.

Ecotourism is on the rise in the Amazon rainforests. People want to experience the rainforest without disrupting it. Tourism creates jobs and generates significant revenue for the regional economy. None of this would be possible without interest in the variety of organisms in this natural environment.

The number of tourists visiting South America has increased as much as 20 percent since 2005. Many of these people come to the continent as ecotourists, exploring the rainforests and other natural areas with minimum impact on the environment.

Human Impact

The loss of trees, or deforestation, for rubber or agriculture has impacted South America's rainforests significantly. During the past 40 years, close to 20 percent of the Amazon rainforest has been lost to these industries. Deforestation causes an "edge effect." When trees are taken down, the forest is more harshly exposed to wind, light, and drier air. This changes the climate in and around the forest and attracts non-native species. Native and endemic populations within the forest must compete with these invading species for food, light, and water. Forest fires are also more likely due to the dry air and the proximity of agricultural and other developed land.

When developing land for agricultural use, people often use slash and burn techniques to clear the area of trees. It is estimated that, in the past 10 years, 10 percent of the Amazon rainforest has been cleared for development purposes.

Conserving Nature

Groups, organizations, and government agencies work together to protect South America. National parks have been formed to conserve the land. Many international conservation and foundation groups are working to save the forest and its wildlife.

In 2007, the Galapagos region was added to the list of World Heritage in Danger sites. Plans were put into action to control tourism and invasive species. So much progress was made that the region was removed from the list. Other groups are making similar progress in preserving the region's marine environment. Natural or historic marine areas are carefully monitored by authorities. This control affects fishing practices and minimizes the disruption of marine life. Some conservationists are working with seafood companies to develop **sustainability** guidelines for the fish they sell.

The Atacama Desert in Chile has one of the clearest skies in the world because the air is so dry. Dry air lacks water vapor and does not hold particles of dirt or dust.

Make an Ecosystem Web

Use this book, and research on the internet, to create a South American ecosystem.

1. Select a South American plant or animal. Think about what habitat it lives in.

2. Find at least three organisms that are found in the same habitat. This could include plants, insects, reptiles, amphibians, birds, fish, and mammals.

3. How do these organisms interact with each other? Do they provide food or shelter for other organisms?

4. Begin linking these organisms together to show which organisms rely on each other for food and shelter.

5. Once your ecosystem web is complete, think about how removing one organism would affect the other organisms in the web.

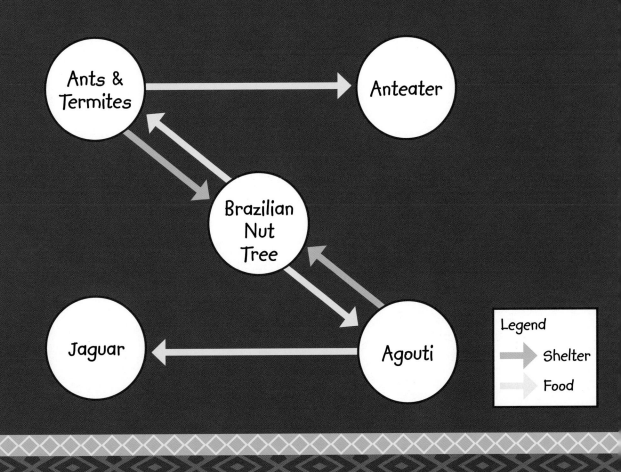

Ants & Termites → Anteater

Ants & Termites ↔ Brazilian Nut Tree

Brazilian Nut Tree ↔ Agouti

Agouti → Jaguar

Legend
→ Shelter
→ Food

Quiz

1 Where is the world's driest place?

The Atacama Desert

2 Name four of South America's land biomes.

Rainforest, grassland, desert, tundra, deciduous forest, and chaparral

3 How many species of insects can be found in South America's rainforest?

More than 2 million

6 How is deforestation threatening South American biomes?

Deforestation is causing the loss of habitats.

4 What is the difference between a freshwater and marine biome?

The amount of salt in the water

5 What is an endemic species?

A species of plant or animal that is found only in one region

7 What percentage of reptiles living on the Galapagos Islands are endemic?

97 percent

9 What do South Americans call their grasslands?

Savannas

8 What landform connects North America and South America?

The Isthmus of Panama

10 Which South American rainforest is the largest in the world?

The Amazon

Key Words

adapt: to change to suit an environment

archipelago: a group of islands

biodiversity: the variety of life in a particular habitat or ecosystem

canopy: the layer of trees at the very top of the rainforest

coral reefs: underwater structures made up of calcium carbonate and populated by marine organisms

echinoderm: an invertebrate spiny-skinned animal

ecotourism: the business of touring natural environments to conserve them

endemic: plant or animal species that are found only in one area

habitats: environments that are occupied by a particular species of plant, animal, or other kind of organism

lomas: islands of vegetation

mangrove: an evergreen tree or bush with entwined roots that are exposed at low tide

photosynthesis: the process plants use to turn carbon dioxide and water into carbohydrates and oxygen using light energy

pollination: the act of transferring pollen from one plant to another which results in fertilization

predators: living by killing and eating other animals

rainforests: forests that receive large amounts of rain and that have very tall trees

species: a group of organisms that share similar characteristics

sustainability: able to maintain nature's balance

vascular: having channels or tubes for carrying fluids

Index

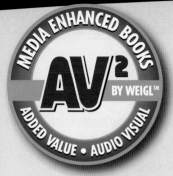

Log on to www.av2books.com

AV² by Weigl brings you media enhanced books that support active learning. Go to www.av2books.com, and enter the special code found on page 2 of this book. You will gain access to enriched and enhanced content that supplements and complements this book. Content includes video, audio, weblinks, quizzes, a slide show, and activities.

AV² Online Navigation

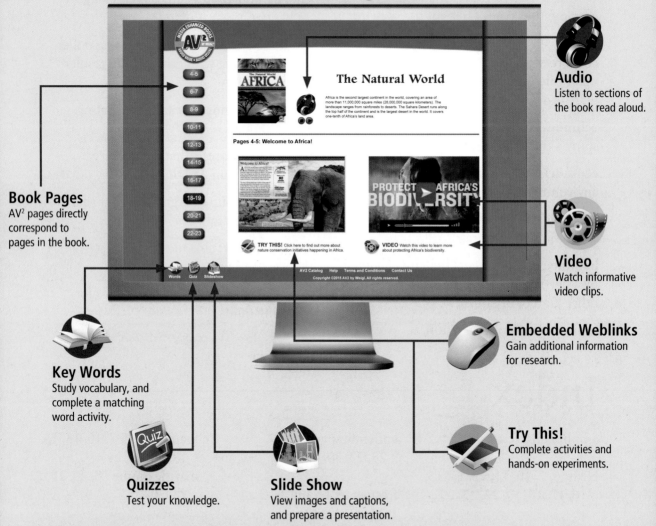

Book Pages
AV² pages directly correspond to pages in the book.

Audio
Listen to sections of the book read aloud.

Video
Watch informative video clips.

Key Words
Study vocabulary, and complete a matching word activity.

Embedded Weblinks
Gain additional information for research.

Quizzes
Test your knowledge.

Slide Show
View images and captions, and prepare a presentation.

Try This!
Complete activities and hands-on experiments.

AV² was built to bridge the gap between print and digital. We encourage you to tell us what you like and what you want to see in the future.

Sign up to be an AV² Ambassador at www.av2books.com/ambassador.

Due to the dynamic nature of the Internet, some of the URLs and activities provided as part of AV² by Weigl may have changed or ceased to exist. AV² by Weigl accepts no responsibility for any such changes. All media enhanced books are regularly monitored to update addresses and sites in a timely manner. Contact AV² by Weigl at 1-866-649-3445 or av2books@weigl.com with any questions, comments, or feedback.